CONTENTS

THE ULTIMATE GUIDE TO
MINECRAFT
2021 EDITION

PAGE 10

Learn all about the essential tools you'll need to get started on your adventure!

PAGE 28

Find out which cool skins to buy for your characters and how to make your own!

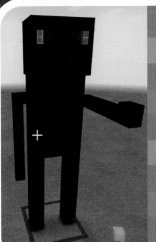

Follow our pro build guides and create five mega Minecraft constructs!

PAGE 32

PAGE 62

Check out all sorts of super secrets lurking in the game!

Published 2020

Little Brother Books Ltd, Ground Floor, 23 Southernhay East, Exeter, Devon, EX1 1QL

Printed in Poland

books@littlebrotherbooks.co.uk
www.littlebrotherbooks.co.uk

Welcome to the world of
MINECRAFT

Released nearly 10 years ago, Minecraft is officially the biggest-selling video game in the world. Millions of players globally have created a mind-boggling variety of levels, characters and constructs, yet barely scratched the surface of what's possible.

MEET THE CREATORS

Minecraft was created by Markus 'Notch' Persson and unleashed on an unsuspecting world in 2011. Jens Bergenstein then took over development of the title for Mojang and various updates and add-ons have only helped to improve Minecraft's playability.

SANDBOX PLAY

Minecraft is essentially one giant sandbox game that allows players to create almost anything they can think of with a variety of resources. Players can choose to explore, mine, build, battle mobs, invent and even act as gods of their own worlds!

LOOKS CAN BE DECIEVING

At first glance Minecraft may appear to be a surprisingly simple game, but it's depths are staggering. Combining world-building, exploration, crafting and character development, Minecraft can also be complex and time-consuming to get to grips with.

SUPER SPIN-OFFS

As well as the main Minecraft game, there have been spin-off titles that have been just as popular. Minecraft: Story Mode, Minecraft Earth and Minecraft Dungeons have all taken the concept in new directions and been huge hits too!

ALL ABOUT THE BLOCKS

On the surface the basic blockiness of Minecraft hides a deceptively sophisticated game. Players are able to collect, combine and create items, ranging from simple building and tools to elaborate bases and complicated gadgets.

GAMING PLATFORMS

Minecraft is available to play on almost every current gaming system. You can try it out on Xbox 360, Xbox One, PlayStation Vita, PlayStation 3, PlayStation 4, Nintendo Switch, Wii U, Nintendo 3DS, PC, Mac, mobile devices and more!

THE ULTIMATE GUIDE

Whether you're a Minecraft noob or a seasoned pro, this Ultimate Guide has something for everyone! We've packed these pages with all sorts of fun information, with help for getting started and basic builds to sneaky secrets and tricky puzzles.

BRILLIANT BUILDS

Looking for some creative inspiration? Then check out our five epic building guides! We'll take you through how to make some really cool Minecraft constructs step-by-step and you can impress your mates with your building skills!

PACKED WITH PUZZLES

As well as hints, tips and guides, this book is also bursting with fun Minecraft puzzles that are sure to test your brain power! The best bit is that the answers to all of the puzzles can be found within these very pages...

TOP 10 YOUTUBERS

Some of the biggest YouTube stars in the world are Minecraft pros. Take a look at our list of the Top 10 YouTubers you should be following and what sort of awesome content their channels have to offer.

GAME MODES

There are a number of different ways to play Minecraft and each of them is fun and challenging. Once you've chosen which platform to play on, it's time to decide if you're going on a solo adventure or with friends.

SINGLE, MULTIPLAYER, REALMS

Single player is the original mode for Minecraft, where you select either Survival or Creative modes. Others can join in on the same console, while Minecraft Realms Plus offers players the ability to set up a server and play online.

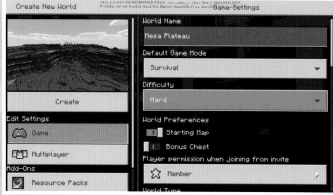

HARDCORE

One for experienced gamers only! In this mode you only have one life as the game is set on the hardest difficulty. If you're killed, it's game over and you'll lose everything you've created and any resources gathered.

SURVIVAL

In this single player mode, you'll have to survive in the world of Minecraft by searching and mining for resources, hunting for food and battling mobs. As you play, you'll also gain valuable experience points.

PEACEFUL

This option is available in Survival mode and lets you build, explore and collect resources without worrying about being attacked by any mobs. As your health also regenerates faster, it's a great option for novice players.

CREATIVE

Sometimes known as god mode, this option allows you to build anything you can imagine via a full inventory. You're also immune from mob attacks, which is handy when travelling to the Nether and the End dimensions.

MINECRAFT REALMS PLUS

This subscription-based service is available on all versions of Minecraft and allows players to create their own servers and host online matches. There are also pre-made world templates, maps and mini-games. Minecraft Realms Plus currently costs £7.99 a month.

YOUR FIRST GAME

When you first start playing in any mode, you'll want to explore the environment you're in to find out what resources are available and what challenges may await. Taking your time and not rushing in could be the difference between life and death!

INVENTORY

When playing in any game mode, players will need to keep an eye on their inventory and ensure it's as fully stocked a possible. This is where you'll need to go to equip armour, weapons and items, craft and more.

THE ADVENTURE BEGINS!

Once you're ready to begin your quest, dive in and prepare to immerse yourself in the world of Minecraft. There's so much to see, do and find, either on your own or with friends, that you're guaranteed to be playing the game for years to come!

TOOLS

One of the very first things you'll need to do when you start a game is to craft some tools. These essential items are needed for all but the most basic of actions and they'll also allow you to mine, build, eat and craft better tools.

CRAFTING TOOLS

All tools first have to be created by finding certain resources and then placing them in the crafting grid in your inventory to create new items. You can find out all about crafting on p14.

BLOCK BUSTER

To begin making tools you'll need to gather the right blocks. To start this will be wood, which can be mined just by using your hands. After a lot of digging in the dirt and chopping down trees you'll be ready to make some tools.

ESSENTIAL ITEMS

There are some basic tools that every adventurer will need in Minecraft. These can be crafted from materials and resources usually found in the local environment. Here are the essentials you'll need to get started:

Pickaxe

Made from wood blocks and used for crafting items

Axe

Made from wood planks and a stick. Handy for defence against mobs

Sword

Made from wood planks and a stick. Kills enemies

Shovel

Made from wood planks and a stick. Needed for digging

Bed

Made from wood planks and wool. Allows you to sleep

Furnace

Made from cobblestone. Used for smelting items

Torches

Made from coal and a stick. Allows you to see in the dark

BETTER TOOLS

Some blocks can only be broken with certain tools. To do that you'll have to craft better versions of your basic tools with stronger elements such as stone, iron, gold and diamond. This also speeds up how long it takes to break blocks apart.

OTHER TOOLS

Some tools are of no use when it comes to breaking blocks, but they're still very useful. These can include such items as hoes, bows, fishing rods, carrots on sticks, flint & steel and buckets.

TIME TO EAT

Once you've crafted a furnace you'll finally be able to cook up some tasty food! To do this you just need to add a fuel source, such as wood or coal, to a furnace along with raw ingredients and you'll soon be a master chef!

CHESTS

As your inventory can only hold a limited number of items, you'll eventually need to craft a chest. These can hold 27 items and two chest placed next to each other can hold double that amount.

ENCHANTED TOOLS

The ultimate way to enhance some tools, weapons and armour is to enchant it. To do this you'll need an enchantment table or anvil, plus certain items to enchant, which results in stronger items with unique properties.

FLINT & STEEL

This incredibly useful tool can be used to light a fire on top of a solid block. It's crafted from an iron ingot and flint and is also required for igniting TNT and Nether portals, plus it can detonate creepers!

BLOCKS

Without Blocks there would be no Minecraft! It's the number one essential ingredient in the game and gives everything its distinctive cube-like appearance. It's possible to break almost every kind of block in the game, collect it and use it for creating.

BLOCK TYPES

There are three different types of block transparency in Minecraft. These are transparent (such as air and water), semi-transparent (such as glass and leaves) and opaque blocks (such as wood and cobblestone).

BREAKING BLOCKS

Players begin the game with only their hands for mining basic blocks like wood and dirt. Tougher blocks require special tools and items such as a pickaxe, shovel, TNT or enchanted tools.

STACK A BLOCK

Once mined, blocks can be collected and used as a resource for building. Placing blocks next to or on top of others allows players to construct almost anything they can think of. The more blocks you have, the more things you can build.

GRAVITY FALLS

It may seem weird, but most blocks in Minecraft actually ignore gravity and will float in the air, even if all other blocks around it have been destroyed. The only exceptions are sand, gravel, anvils, dragon eggs, concrete powder and snow.

BLOCKS NOT BLOCKS

Although all items are referred to as blocks, they're not all actually block-shaped. Slabs, beds, plants, coral, trapdoors, brewing stands and many other items are technically still called blocks, even if they don't look like cubes.

BLOCK TEXTURES

All blocks have textures and colours on them so that players know what items they are picking up. Most textures are static and don't move, but special blocks such as lava, water, prismarine and seagrass have animated textures.

NETHER BLOCKS

Some blocks can only be found by travelling via a portal to the Nether dimension. Netherrack, glowstone and soul sand may be mined here and used for creating light sources, traps and mob spawning.

TNT TIME

One way to harvest a lot of blocks at once is to blow up an area of an environment with TNT. After the explosion there will be lots of blocks waiting to be collected. Some blocks are more easily destroyed than others.

BEDROCK

This type of block is completely indestructible in Survival mode. It's the stuff that the bottom five layers of the Overworld are built out of and these dark blocks can also be found throughout the End.

RARE BLOCKS

Some blocks in Minecraft are super-rare, so good luck finding them! The top 10 rarest blocks are ancient debris, beacon, conduit, diamond ore, dragon egg, emerald ore, gold, ore, lapis lazuli ore, redstone ore and Nether star.

CRAFTING

The world of Minecraft offers players virtually unlimited basic resources, but also the ability to create even more. This is done via crafting and allows multiple items to be combined into new and useful tools, armour, weapons and other items.

INVENTORY MENU

Players can find a small 2x2 crafting grid in their inventory that will allow them to start making simple items and blocks. To create even better items, you'll first need to make a crafting table.

CRAFTING TABLE

Combining four wood planks will create a crafting table. This utility block uses a 3x3 grid system allowing players to combine items into more advanced objects. Placing items in the correct order will then generate the new item.

RECIPE TO SUCCESS

Most versions of the game will now tell you which ingredients are required to craft specific items. With the right items placed in the correct order on the crafting table, it's possible to create a myriad number of new items.

CRAFTING ITEMS

Items that can be crafted range from basics such as tools, food and blocks to more advanced essentials such as dyes, mechanisms and brewing equipment. You'll start at a simple level and learn more complicated recipes as you progress.

RARE RECIPES

There are some lesser-seen items in the game that are fun to craft and create with. Here's a look at some of our favourites:

Glazed terracotta

Stain ordinary terracotta using this recipe to produce a glazed version

Concrete

Combining sand and gravel creates a strong building material

Golden Apple

These delicious magical fruit will regenerate any lost energy

Beacon

Place on top of iron, gold, emerald or diamond pyramid constructs for a beam of light

Sticky piston

An enhanced piston that allows you create push and pull mechanisms

BREWING

Another form of crafting is brewing. This allows players to create special potions that can have all sorts of unique effects. First you'll need to create a brewing stand as shown and then place empty glass bottles into it.

TIME FOR A BREW

You'll also need blaze powder and a water source to begin brewing, as well as Nether wart to create an awkward potion. This basic base potion can then be added to by including other ingredients in the brew.

FIERY FURNACE

Another way of creating useful items is via a furnace. Once crafted, these blocks can be used to cook food and smelt ores. To use the furnace, players need to place fuel and the items they want to smelt into a basic grid.

CHOOSE YOUR SMELTER

Minecraft now includes three different types of smelting block. The smoker is used for food, the blast furnace for ores and the campfire for cooking food. The first two are expensive, but cook much faster than the third.

Mining

The only way to get your hands on many rare and super-useful materials is by mining or digging. As these items are often found well-below ground, you'll need to be properly equipped and prepared before setting off into the caves below the Overworld.

THE RIGHT TOOLS FOR THE JOB

Stock up your inventory with wood for tools, coal for torches and plenty of food for the journey ahead. A bucket of water is also handy for turning lava into obsidian and a furnace is needed for smelting ores.

GOING UNDERGROUND

Digging a hole straight down is a sure way to end up dead. Instead, try to build stairs or spiral staircases to avoid falling into lava, being crushed by falling blocks from above or dropping into caves full of mobs.

LIGHT 'EM UP

Natural light is rare underground, so be sure to craft plenty of torches while you explore. Place these on cave walls to illuminate your way and also to show you the correct path out of an underground area.

LEVEL 32

The most valuable blocks in the game are buried deep underground. The rarest ores only generate below level 32, so you'll need to do some serious digging. Some ores exist as rich strips or veins, so find one and there could be more.

UNDERGROUND MOBS

One of the main hazards of mining are mobs. They're usually lurking in the dark waiting to take you out and include such fiends as skeletons, spiders, zombies, creepers, slimes and others. Keep your eyes peeled!

MINING FOR ORES

Finding these special ores will allow you to craft and create all kinds of useful items in Minecraft. You'll definitely need an iron pickaxe or better to mine these blocks:

Redstone
Make redstone blocks, circuits and mechanisms

Iron
Craft armour, tools, weapons iron blocks, iron golems

Gold
Craft armour, tools, weapons crafting gold blocks

Emerald
Used in villager trading, crafting emerald blocks

Diamond
Craft armour, weapons, tools, diamond blocks, enchantment table

Lapis lazuli
Used as a dye, enchantments, lapis lazuli blocks

Coal
Craft torches, coal blocks, fuel for furnace

Nether quartz
Used for daylight detectors, craft quartz blocks, slabs

Glowstone
Craft glowstone blocks, potion brewing

OBSIDIAN BLOCKS

Usually found at the bottom of a world, where water meets lava and solidifies. A very strong substance that can only be mined with a diamond pickaxe, obsidian is required for creating Nether portals and enchantment tables.

KA-BOOM!

For large-scale mining, you'll need to get your hands on TNT. These blocks can be found naturally in some biomes or crafted using different recipes. Once lit, stand well back as the explosion will take out a huge area!

BASIC BUILDING

You can have all sorts of fun when building in Minecraft and your creations can range from simple structures to elaborate bases. If you're just starting out with the game, it's a good idea to learn the basics before moving on to more complicated builds.

START PLANNING

Before building anything, it's always best to plan out what you're going to create. You could always draw a rough version before starting out, or at least have a general idea of what you're going to be making.

SURVIVAL VS CREATIVE

While it is possible to build in Survival, you have to remember it'll take longer to gather resources and there's always the possibility of mob attacks. You don't have any of those worries in Creative and the sky's the limit!

FLY AWAY

Another great feature of building in Creative mode is that your character has the ability to fly. Soaring through the air allows you to better survey your surroundings and move around the levels much faster.

UNLIMITED RESOURCES

Always wanted to build a solid gold house? Well now you can. In Creative mode you have unlimited resources, which gives you more opportunities to try things out and experiment more with your creations.

BEGINNING CONSTRUCTION

It's a good idea to begin a build by marking out the shape of your building with cobblestone. This will give you a clear idea of how big the structure will be, how many blocks you'll need and how long it'll take to complete.

BUILDING WALLS

Adding walls to your build will help you figure out how tall to make the building, so don't forget to construct it higher than head height! Once the walls are in place you can start to add additional floors above.

ADDING STAIRS

Don't forget to leave room on each floor for stairs. This may seem obvious, but if you forget then you won't be able to move easily between levels. Alternatively, you could add a ladder to reach different rooms.

BASEMENT BELOW

Before you start work on the ground floor of a building, you could always dig down and add a basement area. This subterranean level would be great for storing resources and items, hidden from others.

ATTENTION TO DETAIL

Creating a basic blocky building is very easy, but you can also enhance your creation with more decorative items. Tiles, slabs and stairs are great for the outside of a house, while a fence, gate and plants add nice touches to gardens.

BEGIN AGAIN

Don't worry if a build doesn't quite turn out how you expected the first time around. You can always change, remodel and add to it whenever you want. If it's not possible to salvage your construct, just blow it up with TNT blocks and start again!

GLASS BUBBLE ELEVATOR

When starting out building in Minecraft, you don't have to begin with a huge and complicated construct. Here's a really simple build that looks great and has a very cool feature. Let's get started in Creative mode!

1 First you'll need a large open space to work with. For this build we decided to go with an underground area, which was cleared with plenty of TNT. The different types of blocks and lava make this a dramatic location!

2 Once you have a clear area to get started, it's best to mark out the size of your build. This can be done with any stone blocks or flat slabs placed on the ground. For this build you'll need to lay down a 5x5 grid section.

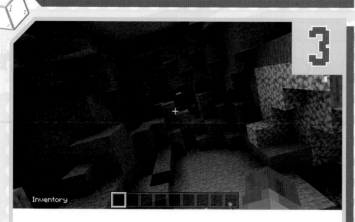

3 Another reason we chose to build a Glass Bubble Elevator underground is that it will take us from the cave floor, right up to the surface of the Overworld. To reach the ground level you'll need to clear all of the blocks above.

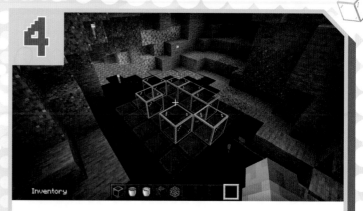

4 Next, you'll need to head to your inventory and stock up on plenty of glass blocks. Place these on top of your marked-out build area in the pattern shown. This first layer of glass blocks marks out the towers you'll be making.

5

It's time to start adding more glass blocks and build vertical towers up to the surface. It's best to start with just one tower at a time so you can check your work at each stage. Keep adding glass blocks until your reach the ground.

6

It's important that each glass tube connects from the base of the elevator up to the Overworld above. Keep checking your progress by looking up to see how far away the ground level is ahead.

7

Once you've made one glass block tower, head back down to the base below and begin construction on the rest of them. In total you'll need to build seven vertical towers to form the main section of the elevator.

8

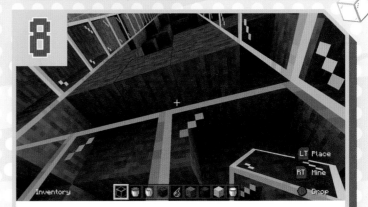

Although plenty of TNT will create a huge cavern for you to work in, you may still encounter blocks getting in your way as your build your glass block towers. If you do, just smash them to clear a path to the surface.

9

Now head up to the Overworld ground level. You'll need to add more glass block to the structure, so that it's clear of the floor. We've built our tower six blocks high above the ground and blocked off a nearby river.

10

Take the time to look down on your build from above and check to see how it's progressing. You may decide to add in more glass blocks to make it taller, or notice that you've missed some blocks on the way up.

Drop all the way down the centre of the construct until you're back in the cave. Inside the base of the elevator, add a couple of signs or fences. These will block off the water you'll be adding next.

Go back into your inventory and select the bucket of water, then head to the top of the first vertical tower and fill it all up. In total there will be two glass tower sections of the elevator that will be filled with water.

Head down to the base of the elevator again and completely fill up the other tower with water. One of the water-filled towers will be the 'up' elevator and the other will be the 'down' elevator.

You've now going to climb back up to the surface. Take this opportunity to make sure that both glass block tubes are totally filled to the top with water. If they're not, just grab your bucket and add some more.

Hop into one of the water-filled tubes and head back down to the base of your elevator build. Then select a block of soul sand from your inventory and place it at the base of the left-hand tower.

Turn around and select a magma block from your inventory. Place this at the base of the right-hand glass block tube. The soul sand will launch you up the tube and the magma will pull you down.

17

Now step back from the glass block elevator tower and admire your handiwork! Make sure that no blocks are missing or that water is leaking from anywhere. Bubbles should be going up and down in the tubes.

18

Return to the surface level again. If you like you can start to build around the exit to your Glass Bubble Elevator to make it look a bit more interesting. We've added grass and dirt blocks around it for definition.

19

Make a show of the entrance to the elevator by adding oak and smooth stone blocks, as well as stone slabs to give it shape. Finally, we added a sign on the front so that visitors to the world will know what it is!

20

Now for the fun part - It's time to test out your elevator! Simply step on to the right-hand water tower and be instantly sucked down the elevator. Step off and try the other tube to whizz to the surface.

21

For some finishing touches, return to the underground section of your build. Add a simple entrance and exit to the elevator with smooth stone blocks. We've also added in a handy door for easy access.

22

For an extra finishing touch, try adding 'Up' and Down' signs inside the base of your elevator. As things can also start to get a little gloomy, we've placed a sea lantern inside to light the way!

Test your Minecraft knowledge on facts you've learnt in this Ultimate Guide!

PUZZLES

MOB SHADOWS

Hostile mobs usually wander around at night and are hard to spot. Take a look at these shadowy outlines and see if you can work out what they are.

1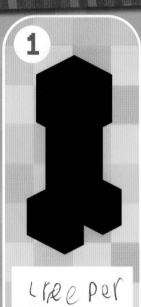

creeper

2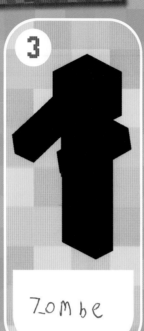

witch

3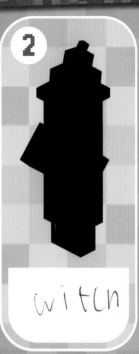

zombe

4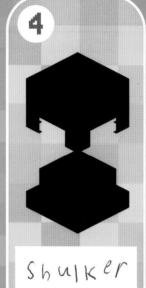

shulker

5

gahst

SLIME SPOT THE DIFFERENCE

These two pictures of slippery slimes may look the same, but the one at the bottom is different. Can you circle all 10 changes that have been made to the slimey picture?

MIXED-UP MOBS

It's time to test your knowledge of Minecraft! Unscramble the names of these mobs and write the correct ones in the blank spaces.

HROOMMOOS

GAVLRLEI

KLRESUH

NROI LGMOE

RAPLO AREB

NNADREEM

YBBA BZEMIO

RELDE NGRAVIDA

THE RWTHEI

RENED RANDGO

MISSING BLOCKS

This awesome Minecraft build is almost complete, but there are some blocks missing. Can you work out where the correct missing blocks go?

1   2   3   4   5

MINECRAFT MAZE

Help Alex make her way safely through this tricky maze and reach the treasure chest at the end. Watch out for explosive creepers along the way!

FINISH

START

Answers on p76

25

Electronics don't exist in the world of Minecraft... enter the miracle material that is Redstone.

REDSTONE

With this extremely versatile substance you'll be able to build amazing gadgets, cool mechanisms and machines of staggering complexity. You'll be a redstone expert in no time!

THE HUNT FOR REDSTONE

You'll initially need to go digging for redstone ore, as it can only be found underground. However, it's also possible to collect six redstone blocks by defeating any witches that you might encounter in Swamp biomes.

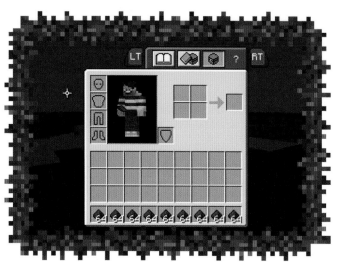

REDSTONE DUST

This substance can transmit a signal from a power source to a redstone component. This will allow you to make circuits and all sorts of stuff. Break down the redstone ore into redstone dust and either smelt or craft it into blocks of redstone.

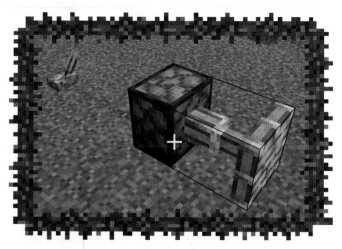

POWERED UP

Redstone dust can be placed on blocks and other items, where it creates a red line (or wire) linking blocks and items together. Placing a power source next to the redstone will cause it to light up and activate, powering your creation.

ENERGY SOURCES

There are lots of ways to power a redstone circuit. These include, switches, levers, pressure plates, tripwires, daylight sensors and more. It's also possible to craft redstone torches and blocks, which can power circuits, too.

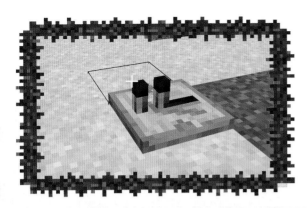

SIGNAL STRENGTH

A redstone signal can usually only travel along 15 blocks, unless it receives a boost from another power source along the way. A redstone repeater can be crafted that allows signals to be turned on and off, amplified, delayed or locked.

REDSTONE CRAFTING

Use your redstone resources to craft these useful items and take your constructs to another level:

Observer
Emits a signal when the block it's monitoring is updated

Dropper
Can be used to push items into another container

Dispenser
Items can be dispensed from this block when activated

Clock
A simple device that displays the current in-game time

Powered rail
A special rail used to speed up or slow down minecarts

Detector rail
Can detect when minecarts are on it and how full they are

Note block
These musical blocks begin to play when powered up

Redstone lamp
Blocks that light up when activated with a redstone signal

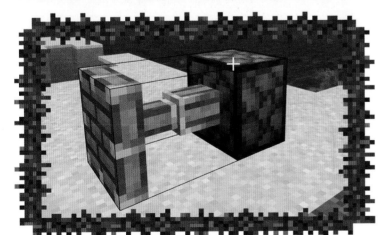

PISTONS AND STICKY PISTONS

Once you've learned the basics of redstone, you can start building pistons. These blocks can push other blocks as part of mechanisms and can also be turned into sticky pistons, which stick to blocks when extended.

SLIME BLOCKS

Use slimeballs to craft slime blocks and attach the block to a redstone-powered sticky piston. You'll be able to grab and move other blocks around and they can also be used as springy platforms.

CHARACTER SKINS

One of the great creative features of Minecraft is the ability for players to customise the look of their own character or skin. By giving character's their own unique appearance, players can show off their creative skills to others!

STARTER SKINS

When you first begin a game, you can only choose from one of two basic starter skins. These are called Steve and Alex and represent a male and a female character. The skins are 1.8 blocks tall and 0.6 blocks wide.

CREATE A CHARACTER

Select the character profile button on the main menu and you'll be taken to the Character Creator page. From here you'll be able to change almost any aspect of your look with free or paid-for items.

HEADS, SHOULDERS, KNEES AND TOES

On the Character Creator page, players have a range of options available for changing their character's hair, head, face, body arms, legs and more. It's also possible to apply different colours to each for a one-of-a-kind look.

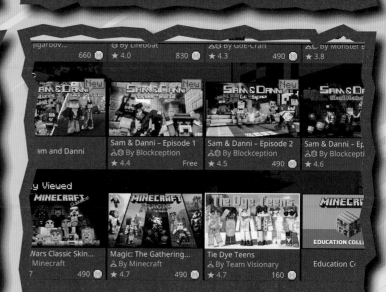

SPENDING MINECOINS

If you want even more options, you'll need to splash some cash. A huge range of items are available to purchase from the Minecraft Marketplace, but will require you to spend Minecoins.

SKIN PACKS

These downloadable extras are available to buy in the Minecraft Marketplace. There are all sorts of amazing skins to purchase including many famous ones from video games, movies, TV shows and more.

THE BEST SKIN PACKS

There are loads of cool skins to grab from the Marketplace, but some of our favourites are the *Star Wars*, *Power Rangers*, *Magic: The Gathering* and *Minecraft Story Mode* packs. Go check them out!

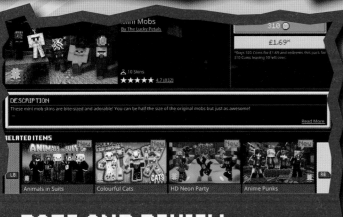

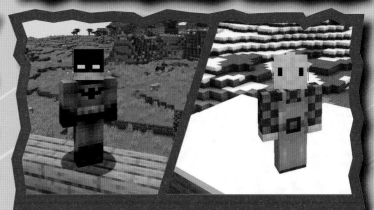

RATE AND REVIEW

Too many skins to choose from? Minecraft Marketplace has reviews of everything to buy, with star ratings and comments on each item that will help you decide whether you should spend your Minecoins on them.

FAN-MADE SKINS

Some Minecraft players have created their own incredible skins that you can download. There are lots out there to try and some of our favourites include Batman, Elsa, Bob the Builder, Iron Man and Darth Maul!

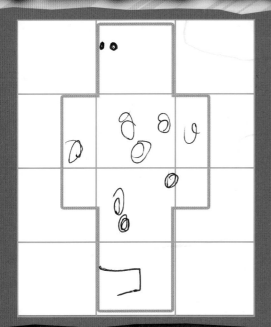

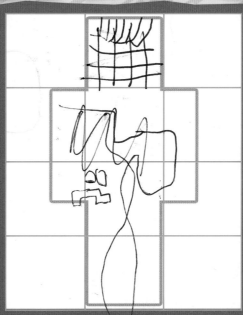

DESIGN YOUR OWN SKINS

Use these blank templates to design your own Minecraft skin, and then try and create them in the game!

BIOMES

When you begin a game in Minecraft you'll spawn into a new world or biome. There are lots of different and unique environments to explore and mine, with each region having its own challenges, resources and mobs. Let's start exploring!

DESERT

There's very little to see and find in these dusty biomes, with few resources or water. Go mining to grab rare fossils.

SAVANNA

Dry and flat, Savannas are home to villagers and horses. There's no rain at all, so farming can prove to be a bit tricky.

EXTREME HILLS

Building and exploring can be quite treacherous in these biomes, but they're also the only ones to contain emerald ore.

FOREST

The ideal starting biome, these environments are rich in trees and grass. Perfect for building your first home in relative safety.

ROOFED FOREST

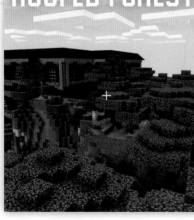

Covered in dense tree canopies, roofed forests often hide hostile mobs in their gloom, so keep an eye out.

JUNGLE

Although tricky to build in, jungles are rich in resources. They're also home to exclusive items such as melons and cocoa.

ICE PLAINS

Flat and snowy biomes, ice plains are quite tough to survive in. However, they are handy for sugar cane, and other items.

Another biome that's easy to build in. Plains are flat and covered in grass, with villages of all sizes dotted throughout.

PLAINS

Not the most hospitable of building conditions, but trees and water are in abundance. Watch out for slimes and witches though!

SWAMP

OCEAN

Rich in resources, oceans are also tricky to live in and on. Diving further into their depths reveals ancient temples and monuments.

MESA

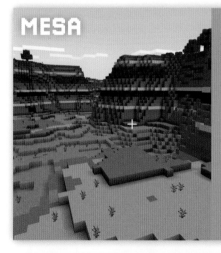

With very little resources, these biomes are made up of hardened clay, red sand trees. Go mining and you'll find lots of gold.

Covered in spruce trees, taiga biomes are a great environment for beginners to learn how to build and gather resources.

TAIGA

There's no way to spawn in this biome, but learn how to build a special portal and you can explore this dangerous dimension.

THE NETHER

THE END

The final challenge for only the bravest players, this biome is also only accessible via building a portal. Can you beat the Ender Dragon?

GIANT ENDERMAN

For this build we're going to create a monster-sized version of a Minecraft mob from The End. The giant Enderman may look simple to make, but it actually has a lot of cool hidden features too.

1

To begin constructing the Enderman, we've chosen a super flat biome, but you can build yours in any kind of world. To match the colour of the mob's skin, we suggest going for black wool or obsidian blocks.

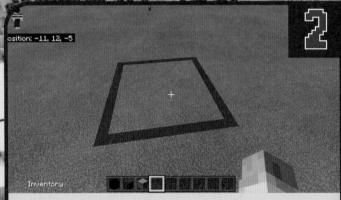

2

Now clearly mark out an area to place your build within. This will also help you work out how large the Enderman figure will be and how many blocks you'll need. You can make the building area any size you like.

3

Next you'll want to move on to making one of the Enderman's feet. Build the first foot towards the edge of the marked out area and place a 3x3 grid of black wool blocks on the ground, one block high.

4

Go to the other side of the marked out area and place a 3x3 grid on the opposite side for the other foot. Again, this will be one block high. Now move back slightly to check you're happy with the position of both feet.

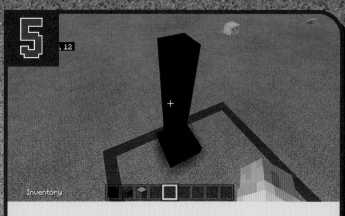

5

With the Enderman's feet complete, you can now start construction on the figure's left leg. Build vertically with the black wool blocks and make sure that each leg is 20 blocks high from the ground up.

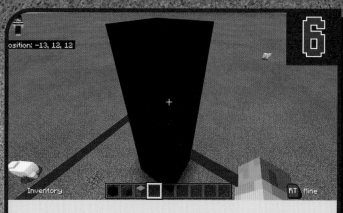

6

Move around the left leg and add vertical black wool blocks up from each of the feet. Do this for all the blocks until you have a 20 block tall tower. Now hollow out the centre of the leg, down to the ground.

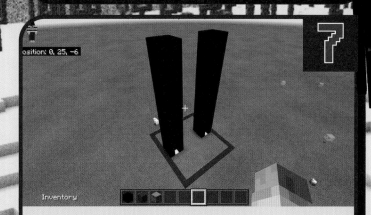

7

With the left leg finished, it's now time to move onto the right. As before, add black wool blocks from the feet upwards, so that you end up with 20 block columns all the way round. Hollow out the middle blocks too.

8

Head to the base of one of the legs. Hollow out a door space four or five blocks in height. This will allow you access to the hollowed out centre section. Place a sea lantern in the ground and repeat on the other leg.

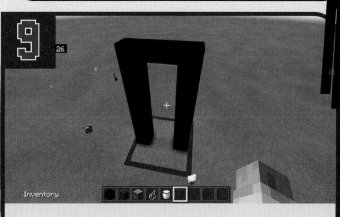

9

The basic construction of the legs is now complete, so it's time to join them both together. Use more black wool blocks to connect one leg to the other. These are the hips of the Enderman and the start of its body.

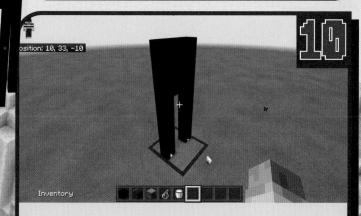

10

Add lots more black wool blocks to the hips and slowly start to build up the Enderman's body. It's always a good idea to move around whatever you're making, just to see if there are any gaps or missed blocks.

11

Let's begin work on the Enderman's head. To start with, we've made it just one block deep to help work out the correct size and shape, which should be the same width as the body. Move back to check it looks right.

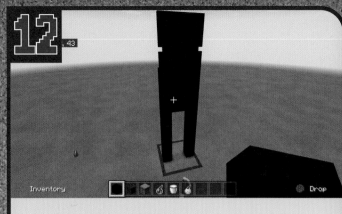

12

To join the Enderman's head to its body, you'll need to add in a neck. The best way to do this is to place a line of black wool blocks the entire length of the head and then remove one block at each end.

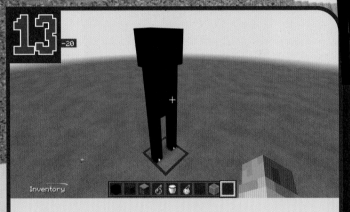

13

We're now going to add some depth to the front and back of the head to make it look like a giant cube. Place more black wool blocks on either side and then zoom out to check everything looks good.

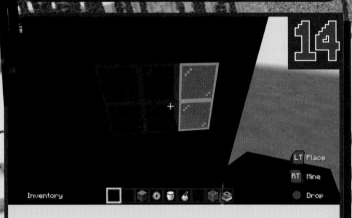

14

For the next part of the build we're going to add in the Enderman's iconic spooky eyes! These can be achieved by placing purple and clear glass blocks into the 3x2 grid as shown. Start with one eye first.

15

When you're happy with the look and placement of one of the Enderman's eyes, move over to the other side of its head to make the other. Again, use the coloured glass blocks, but flip their placement.

16

With the head and eyes complete, it's now time to move on to the left arm. For this one, we're going to place black wool blocks sticking out from the Enderman's body with a small platform at the end.

17

Go to the other side of the body and add in the right arm. This one should be pointing straight down to the ground. To avoid the arm being placed right next to the body, build it one block out from the shoulder.

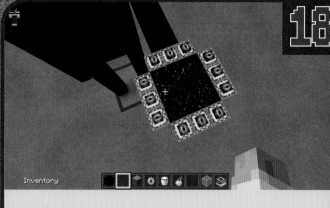

18

At the end of the left arm, we're going to add in a very cool touch. This will be a handheld portal to the End, made from End portal frame blocks and 12 x eyes of Ender. Place them in the correct order to activate it.

19

Head back down to the back of the left leg. As with Build # 1, we're going to add in a bubble elevator. Place a block of soul sand inside, as well as two sign blocks. Fill the inside with water for the 'up' elevator.

20

Now go over to the back of the right leg. To make the 'down' elevator, simply add a magma block inside it at the base and two sign blocks. Fill this leg with water as well to allow quick travel to the ground level.

21

With the outside finished, go inside the head and turn it into a mini base! This can be a handy place to store items and treasures. Don't forget to dig down and link up the head to your bubble elevator.

22

Now your giant Enderman build is complete! You can use this towering terror to impress your mates, hide from your enemies and access the End via the handy portal. If you want, you could make it even larger!

Test your Minecraft knowledge on facts you've learnt in this Ultimate Guide!

PUZZLES

MAKE A CREEPER MASK

Spook your friends with this awesome creeper face! Simply follow the instructions below to make your very own Minecraft mob mask.

1. If you haven't read page 35, scan and print this page and then cut around the dotted lines
2. Stick it on to a piece of stiff card
3. Cut around the mask and cut out the eye and side holes
4. Thread string through the side holes and tie a knot
5. Wear your mask like a true creeper!

HIDDEN HEROBRINE

You never know if you'll encounter Herobrine in Minecraft, so always keep your eyes peeled! Take a look at this picture and see if you can spot him hiding.

BLOCK SEQUENCE

Look carefully at each sequence below and then work out which block comes next. Write the letters in the blank boxes.

 A

1

 **B**

2

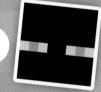 **C**

3

TOO MANY CHICKENS!

Chickens sure can multiply quickly in Minecraft, so it's hard to keep track of them! Take a look at this picture and see how many you can spot.

UNDERWATER

Ocean biomes are some of the most amazing worlds to explore and build in, but they're not without a number of challenges. Here's what you should be looking out for and doing when adventuring in the inky depths of the deep.

UPDATE AQUATIC

Since this addition to Minecraft, players can now explore a variety of underwater biomes. These include lukewarm, cold, frozen and warm oceans, with each spawning different mobs to encounter.

STAYING ALIVE

Unlike other biomes, it's impossible to survive underwater unless you're able to breath. Collect scutes from turtles and use them to craft turtle shells, which can then be used as a helmet, or carry potions of water breathing.

SO MUCH SEA LIFE

There are all sorts of incredible mobs living underwater, from fish and dolphins to squid and guardians. As well as being a source of food, many of these creatures can be used to craft weapons, clothing and other handy items.

FISHING BY BOAT

The fastest way travel on water is by boat. This will increase your speed, save your energy and avoid you being attacked by guardians. While on a boat, use a fishing road to catch all kinds of tasty and useful mobs.

BUILDING UNDERWATER

If you're going to build a submerged construct, try to place it towards the edge of the ocean biome. This will then give you access to useful resources from both the surrounding land and water areas.

FROZEN OCEAN BIOME

This most extreme ocean variant, these biomes are the only place you'll find icebergs. It also snows here instead of raining and the only way to reach water is to dig through the ice. There are even deep frozen biomes to be found...

SHIPWRECKS AHOY!

Included as part of Update Aquatic, shipwrecks are underwater structures made of wood blocks that can contain a number of treasure chests. Other items found in shipwrecks can include TNT, coal, food, maps and more.

OCEAN MONUMENTS

Splash Potion of Night Vision
Night Vision (6:00)

These massive underwater structures are usually built from prismarine blocks and lit internally by sea lanterns. In the centre of a monument is a treasure chest containing gold blocks and guarded by deadly guardians and elder guardians!

SPONGE BLOCKS

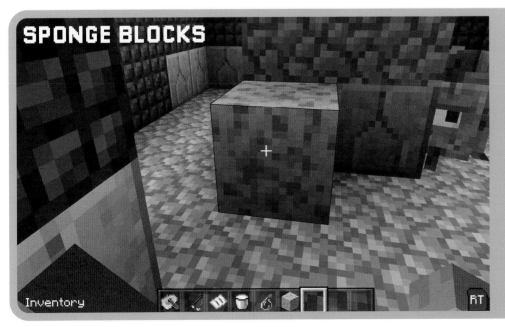

Grab wet sponges from an ocean monument and dry them in a furnace. You can then use the dried sponge blocks to soak up water blocks that may need removing from a level, which is handy when building underwater.

FARMING

You can find all kinds of tasty food in the Overworld, but there's a better way to get all of the grub that you want. Setting up a farm allows you to grow sustainable crops and raise animals without having to venture past your own house.

FEED 'EM AND BREED 'EM

Start by building a simple 10x10 pen to keep your animals in and to protect them. You'll also need to keep feeding them with the snacks they like. If you have two or more of the same animal, they'll eventually have babies.

DYEING SHEEP'S WOOL

Try dyeing your sheep before they breed and you'll end up with all sorts of crazy colours. You can use some flowers for dyes, plus lapis lazuli, ink sacs, cocoa beans and cactus.

CROP FARMING

Begin your farm with a flat area of dirt blocks. Craft an iron hoe and till the blocks before planting anything. It's also handy to have a water source running through your farm.

BONE MEAL

Planting crops will allow them to grow over time, but there's a much faster method for boosting your Minecraft harvest. Try using bone meal on crops, as it's a fantastic fertiliser.

CARROTS, POTATOES, BEETROOT AND WHEAT

These are all dependable crops that are easy to grow. You can obtain them from local village farms and plant them in the prepared dirt. Only harvest them when they reach full maturity.

MELONS & PUMPKINS

Prepare some dirt and plant pumpkin and melon seeds. They don't need water to grow and a stem will appear, then a melon or pumpkin next to it. Harvest your crop and leave the stem to repeat the process.

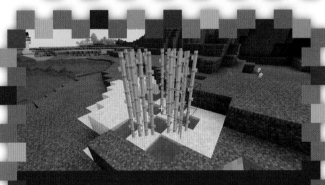

SUGAR CANE

This crop is really useful as it can be eaten and used for baking and making paper. You'll need to plant sugar cane on dirt, grass or sand blocks that are next to a water blocks to allow them to flourish.

MUSHROOMS

They may not be to everyone's taste, but mushrooms can be grown in areas where the light level is less than 12. Plant them and they'll quickly grow and flourish on nearby blocks.

FOODS FOR BREEDING

Here are the various different types of food you'll need to gather to keep your animals well-fed:

Sheep
Wheat

Cow
Wheat

Mooshroom
Wheat

Pig
Carrots, potatoes, beetroot

Horse
Golden apples, golden carrots

Tamed wolf
Any raw meat, any cooked meat

Cat
Raw cod, raw salmon, clownfish, pufferfish

Rabbit
Dandelions, carrots, golden carrots

Chicken
Seeds, pumpkin seeds, melon seeds, beetroot seeds

BUILD #3

OCEAN BASE

There's nothing more satisfying in Minecraft than creating your own secret base. Instead of placing ours on land though, we're going to dive deep under the sea for a cool build that will really show off your creative skills!

1

To start with, hop into Creative mode and choose a suitable biome. While you can always make an underwater base in a world that has rivers and lakes, we've decided to select an ocean biome for deeper water.

2

Our build actually begins on dry land with an entrance to the base. This is a simple structure made from prismarine, prismarine blocks and dark prismarine, as well as sea lanterns to light it all up.

3

Here's the completed entrance to the ocean base. Ours is a basic 5x4 cube shape, with prismarine slabs on the roof to complete it. You can make yours as complicated or as simple as you like and add decorations.

4

Next we're going to need to start digging down to the ocean floor below. Hollow out the floor inside your entrance to make a handy spiral staircase. These steps will be made out of prismarine slabs.

5

The lower down you go, the darker everything is going to get. You can use torches or a night vision potion to light your way, but we've decided to add a central column of sea lanterns all the way down the staircase.

6

Another option for getting down to the sea floor level is to build a more straightforward staircase. This version also uses prismarine slabs and sea lanterns, but just goes in a straight line to the seabed instead.

7

Once you've tunnelled down and reached the bottom, take a good look around. This will be the area where you'll be building your main base. Make sure to clear out any blocks, plants and mobs you may find.

8

From the point you emerge into the ocean, start building a short tunnel out to your base. This can be constructed from prismarine blocks and clear glass, so that you can see out into the surrounding water.

9

Now it's time to mark out the floor area for your submerged base. We've created this with a 9x9 grid of prismarine. You can make the floor as large or as small as you like, as long as it's completely flat.

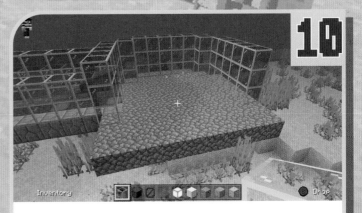

10

Start extending the walls of the tunnel and build them up from the prismarine base. Keep using clear glass blocks, and make the walls three blocks high. You could also use some solid blocks if you like.

11

With the glass block walls in place, we've decided to make them look a little more interesting than a just simple cube. Try taking out the corner sections of the walls and moving them in to the base slightly.

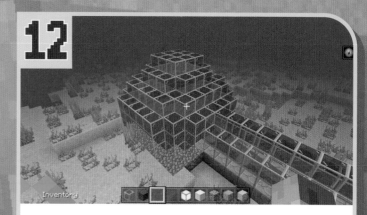

12

To complete the main build of your underwater hideaway, you'll need to add the roof section on top. Use lots of clear glass blocks to build up layers for the roof, giving it a sort of pyramid shape.

13

Head back inside your base by smashing a glass block and repairing it, or head to the surface entrance. Once inside you'll need to clear out all of that ocean water by placing some sponges around the place.

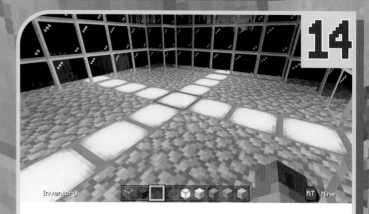

14

Now we're going to start work on the main interior section of the base. To begin with, add sea lanterns in a pattern on the floor. This will light up the room and is also a really cool way to decorate.

15

Turn around inside the room and look back down the short corridor that connects it to the land. Add in a few more sea lanterns to light your way for when you make the journey back to the stairs and surface.

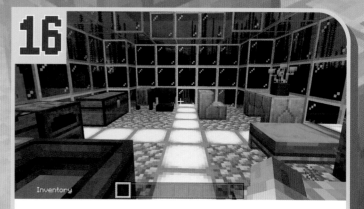

16

Complete the interior decoration of your base by adding in all of the items you like. Handy things to include could be chests, a crafting table, furnace, chairs, a bed, sink, plants and more.

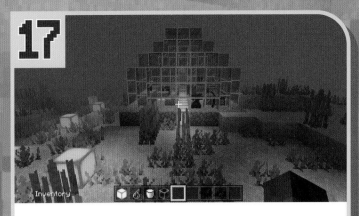

17 Of course, it can be quite dark and gloomy outside your ocean base, so you might want to light up the area with sea lanterns. Not only does this look impressive, but it allows you to view the sea life outside.

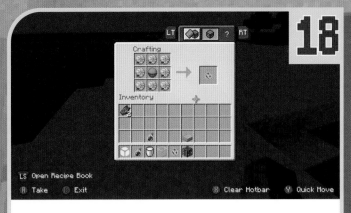

18 Another way of creating light when underwater is to build a conduit construct. For this you'll need to collect eight sea of nautilus shells and a heart of sea and combine them in the crafting grid as shown.

19 Next, head back into the sea and select a clear area near your base. Use prismarine blocks to create a basic 5x5 frame shape. You can build and place as many of these as you like all around the sea floor.

20 Place a glass block on the middle bottom of the frame and then place the conduit block on top of it. Now remove the glass block so that the conduit block is floating above the prismarine frame.

21 Build horizontal and vertical frames all around the main prismarine frame. Once completed, the conduit block will light up, providing plenty of illumination in the area, allowing you to see in the murky depths.

22 For a finishing touch, try adding coral blocks and other plant structures around your base. This will give your build a truly aquatic feel and the plant life will attract all sorts of interesting underwater mobs!

Test your Minecraft knowledge on facts you've learnt in this Ultimate Guide!

PUZZLES

How well do you know your biomes? Take a look at these four images and see if you can identify each of them. Write your answers in the spaces.

(A) ice pains

(B) mushroom ice land

(C) mesa

(D) desert

CRAFTING RECIPES

Look at the three recipes below and see if you can correctly identify which item will be made from each set of ingredients.

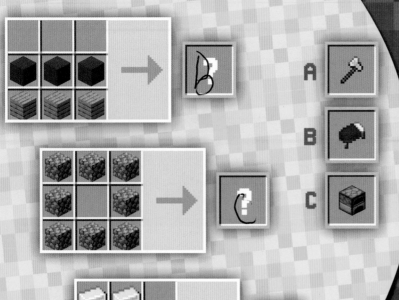

A

B

C

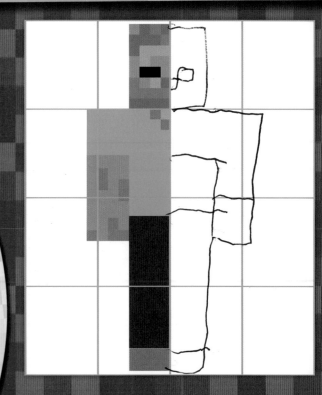

ZOMBIE DRAWING

Complete this picture of a zombie by copying what's in the boxes on the left into the blank spaces on the right. When you've finished, you can colour in the image!

WHICH WITCH?

Can spot which of these spooky witches is the odd-one-out?
They make all look scary and the same, but one of them is different.

MOB MEMORY GAME

The best Minecraft players need to have a good memory if they want to survive!
Study this picture for 60 seconds, cover it and try to answer as many questions as possible.

1. How many torches are there?

2. Where in the picture are the brown dirt blocks?

3. Which two mobs are there only one of?

4. How many zombie faces can you see?

---

1. 6

2. they are on the left pictcur

3. The spider and the wither sckelton

4. I can see 2

Answers on p76

MOBS

The world of Minecraft is inhabited by all manner of creatures known as mobs (short for 'mobile'). Some of them are harmless and will help you in your quests, whiles others are deadly and must be avoided at all costs!

PASSIVE MOBS

Usually found throughout the Overworld, passive mobs can be defeated with basic weapons and tools, providing players with useful items and meat for food. Chickens, sheep, pigs, rabbits, cows and llamas are all passive mobs.

NEUTRAL MOBS

These won't attack you unless they're provoked! If they do, you'll have to kill them with whatever weapons you have to hand. Neutral mobs include wolves, polar bears, spiders and Endermen. Wolves can also be tamed by feeding them tasty bones.

HOSTILE MOBS

You'll definitely need to watch your back in Minecraft as these mobs are lurking everywhere. While many can be found underground during the day others, such as zombies and creepers, will spawn at night to attack.

BOSS MOBS

There are only two boss mobs in the game and they're tough as nails. The Wither can be created by players and will attack anything it sees, while the Ender Dragon is found flying around the End waiting to be challenged.

SPAWNING

Most mobs can spawn in all sorts of locations depending on the right conditions. Some can spawn baby versions of themselves, while other mobs, such as iron golems and The Wither must be made by players.

VILLAGERS

Classed as passive mobs, villagers are to be found throughout the Overworld and have various special skills and professions. They usually gather together in villages and are handy for trading with, if you're after certain items.

ILLAGERS

Although resembling friendly villagers, these mobs are definitely hostile and will attack players on sight. They include the evoker, illusioner, pillager, ravager and vindicator and vex and groups of them often have their own leaders.

UNDEAD MOBS

Some of the most dangerous mobs in Minecraft, these creatures require special items to defeat them. Potions of Healing, Harming or Fire Resistance will usually work. All undead mobs sink in water, if you can lure them into it.

UNDERWATER MOBS

Even the deep blue ocean biomes are packed with mobs! When heading underwater, make sure to keep your eyes peeled for dolphins, squids, turtles, pufferfish and more aquatic creatures, but beware the guardians and powerful elder guardians.

X-RAY VISION

Did you know there are a handful of hostile mobs that can actually see through walls? These include spiders, cave spiders, slimes, silverfish, illusioners. Even solid blocks won't hide you from these critters!

TOP 10 MINECRAFT RAREST MOBS

The world of Minecraft is inhabited with all kinds of animals, creatures and entities, known as mobs. Some are helpful and essential to you progressing through the game, while others are out to end your adventures for good. Which of the top 10 rarest mobs can you find?

10 RED AND BROWN MOOSHROOMS

Red mooshrooms only spawn in the Mushroom island biome, making them rare. However, there is a rarer brown variant that only appears when a red mooshroom is struck by lightning!.

9 ENDERMAN-CREATED GOLEMS

It's possible to get an Enderman to help you create iron golems and snow golems. Make an enclosed area with a golem body and pumpkins. Spawn lots of Endermen and they might pick up a pumpkin and place it on the body for you.

8 TROPICAL FISH

There are 2700 different variations of tropical fish in Minecraft, based on size, colour or patterns. That means one unique fish has a 1/2700 chance of existing, which only happens 10% of the time. Phew!

7 WANDERING TRADER VILLAGER

This mob has a slim chance of spawning into the game every 20 minutes of real time, but this increases every 20 minutes up to a 7.5%. Once it appears, the wandering trader villager often has some unique items.

6 SKELETON TRAPS

Only appearing during lightning storms, a skeleton trap has a chance of spawning based on your difficulty level. If it works, four skeleton horsemen will appear with enchanted gear, along with skeleton horses. Spooky!

5 SHEEP

Yep, it's true. While white sheep are the most common, rarer versions include black, grey, light grey and brown can also be found. Rarer still is the pink sheep variant, which is almost impossible to find!

4 ENDERMITES

When throwing an ender pearl, there's a very slim chance that an endermite may appear. Be careful though as when they do spawn in, these little critters will attack you straight away.

3 QUADRUPLET CHICKENS

Although found naturally in Minecraft, there's a 1/8 chance of spawning a baby chicken by throwing an egg. Even rarer than that are when four baby chickens spawn at once. That almost never happens!

2 SPIDER JOCKEYS

A skeleton riding on a giant spider may sound scary, but the chances of actually seeing one in the game are actually super-rare. Variants include the regular skeleton, wither skeleton and stray skeleton.

1 CHICKEN JOCKEYS

If you thought that spider jockeys were rare, then check out the spider jockey! Spawn a baby zombie, baby husk, baby zombie villager, baby zombie pigman or baby drowned near chickens and they'll ride them!

THE NETHER

It's time to leave the green hills and forests of the Overworld as we travel to a nightmarish realm filled with hostile mobs and valuable items. In June 2020 Mojang released the Nether Update, which added all sorts of cool new stuff to the game!

THROUGH THE PORTAL

To reach The Nether, you'll first need to build a special portal. This can be constructed using 10 obsidian blocks arranged in a frame as shown. Stand in the frame and use flint and steel to activate a swirling vortex to be transported to the Nether.

GEAR UP

Before you travel, make sure you've outfitted yourself with the best equipment that you have. Enchanted diamond armour and weapons are a must, as well as plenty of potions for Healing. Even with all of those items, prepare to die... a lot!

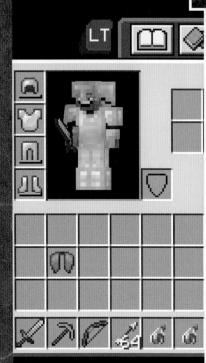

NETHER FORTRESSES

Although this fiery dimension doesn't have many distinguishing features, there are huge Nether fortresses to be found. Packed with vicious mobs, these locations are rich in loot and materials to grab.

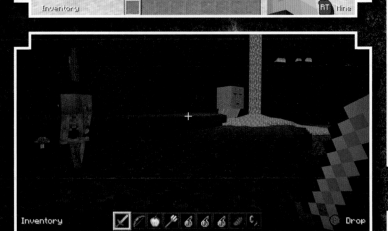

SURVIVE AND EXPLORE

Once you've arrived, you'll notice there's lava everywhere, so watch your step! The Nether contains dangerous cliffs, lethal mobs and magma blocks. To avoid dying too soon, build a shelter around the portal, which will also mark where to return to once you're ready to exit.

NETHER FARMING

It is actually possible to grow things in the Nether and even take animals with you. Crops such as mushrooms, wheat, carrots, potatoes and beetroot will flourish, but other plants will require you take water with you in a bucket.

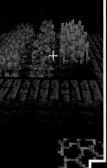

MINING IN THE NETHER

There are many unique blocks to be found in the Nether that can be used for building back in the Overworld. These include the following:

Nether brick   Netherrack   Glowstone   Netherite

Nether wart   Soul sand   Nether quartz ore   Target Block

MOB MAYHEM

The residents of the Nether don't take kindly to strangers trespassing, so watch out! Defeat these malicious mobs to collect special items:

Blaze
Drops: Blaze rod, glowstone

Piglins
Drops: Golden sword, crossbow, golden armour

Ghost
Drops: Ghast tear, gunpowder

Wither skeleton
Drops: Coal, bones, skull, sword

Magma cube
Drops: Magma cream

Zombie piglin
Drops: Rotten flesh, gold nugget, gold ingot, golden sword

Hoglins
Drops: Raw porkchop, cooked porkchop, leather

The Wither
Drops: Nether star

THE END

All of your adventures have led you to this ultimate challenge — the End. Be prepared to enter a strange new dimension, discover rare items, battle bizarre foes and face off against the deadliest Minecraft boss mob!

TRAVEL TO THE END

This unique realm can only be accessed by locating hidden underground strongholds. There are 128 of these per world, so craft eyes of ender (using the recipe shown) to find them. Place 12 eyes of ender on to the portal frame to activate it.

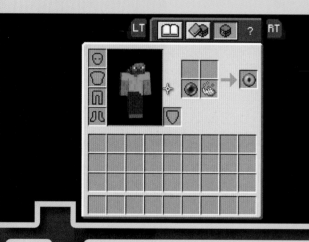

PACK FOR ADVENTURE

Wearing enchanted diamond armour is recommended, as well as equipping a shield, enchanted diamond sword and pickaxe. Potions of Healing, Swiftness and Strength will come in handy, plus try the feather falling enchantment on your boots.

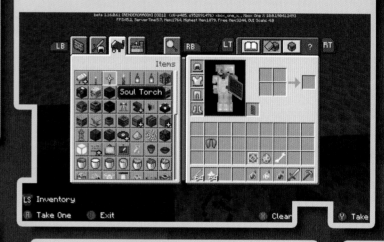

END ENVIRONMENT

As soon as you arrive, you'll notice the End is made up of one large island surrounded by smaller islands floating in the endless nothingness of the void. Although there are various mobs to battle and End cities to explore, you'll just want to head to the main island.

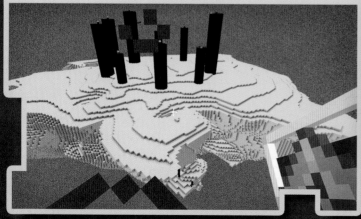

THE ENDER DRAGON

There's no way out of this shadowy dimension unless you defeat this ultimate boss mob! The Ender Dragon constantly flies around the main island, protecting the podium in the centre and drawing power from the crystals on top of obsidian pillars.

DRAGON SLAYER

It's incredibly tough to beat the Ender Dragon, but it can be done. Destroy the crystals first, either from the ground or by building blocks up to them. Use arrows from a distance against the dragon and when it drops down on to the podium, hit it with your sword and splash potions of Harming to defeat it.

THE ULTIMATE PRIZE

Beat the Dragon and you'll be rewarded with 12,000 experience points and the legendary Dragon egg. However, if you try to mine it, the egg will teleport away! Place blocks around the egg and use a piston to push it off for collection.

END MOBS

You can find mobs wandering the islands and lurking in sprawling End cities. Defeat them and you'll pick up some unique rewards:

Shulker

Drops: Shulker shell

Enderman

Drops: Ender pearl

Ender Dragon

Drops: Dragon egg

THE END AND BEYOND

Beat the Dragon and two portals appear. One takes you back to the Overworld and the other leads to the outer islands for more exploration. Choose the exit and you'll get to read the End Poem, which lasts over nine minutes!

BUILD #4

REDSTONE CHEST TRAP

It's time to get a bit more complicated with your Minecraft builds! Adding simple redstone features can really enhance your constructs and also be used to hide some very sneaky little booby traps...

1

Create a new world and choose Creative mode. For this build we've gone for a fairly flat desert biome, with plenty of space all around. You could build yours anywhere though and even use the terrain to hide it away.

2

We're going to start with a couple of sticky pistons. Add one on top of another, then place a couple of iron blocks next to the pistons. Repeat on the other side, with a space of two blocks in-between.

3

Next you'll want to add more iron blocks. Place four blocks on top to link up the ones attached to the sticky pistons, then add a few on each side to match each other. Move back slightly to check your progress.

4

Now we're going to start adding the items that will allow the doors to open and close. Place a line of redstone dust running from the left sticky piston down across the iron blocks on the outside of the build.

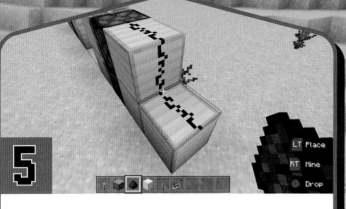

5

Then head over to the other side of the build and add more redstone dust from the sticky pistons on that side, across the iron blocks. Don't forget, if you don't add enough redstone dust, the doors won't work.

6

Go to the left-hand side again and place three iron blocks in the ground, in front of the build. Then place more redstone dust on top of the blocks from the outer edge of the build-up to the sticky pistons.

7

Repeat the same number of iron blocks and redstone dust to the right-hand side of the build, so that it matches the left. Once that's completed, zoom out to check that both sides mirror each other.

8

With the side redstone circuits in place move to the top of the build and look down. You'll need to add a line of redstone dust to all the iron blocks, linking up the redstone dust circuits on either side.

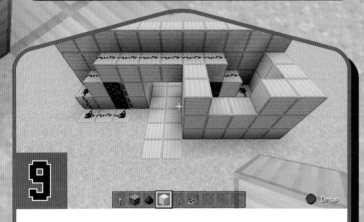

9

Use more iron blocks to cover up the front and back of the build and hide away all of the redstone dust. This looks neater and also disguises the fact that there is more to this construct than meets the eye!

10

On the front right-hand side of the build, add a lever and make sure the block is connected to the redstone dust circuit inside. You can always remove blocks to check that everything is lined up correctly.

11

If you've placed redstone in the right places, one flick of the lever should activate the sliding door mechanism. If it doesn't, simply remove some of the iron blocks and double check all of the connections.

12

Now for the really sneaky part! Place an empty treasure chest part way inside the tunnel. Then dig underneath the chest and place a bunch of TNT blocks and redstone dust up to the iron blocks above.

13

Once your booby trap is all set up, cover up the hole with more iron blocks and place a couple of pressure plates on top. From a distance everything will look safe, but just make sure you don't step on the plates!

14

Head round to the back of the build and make the same sliding doors mechanism as you did at the front. For this you'll need iron blocks attached to sticky pistons, with redstone dust circuits linking them.

15

Add in a lever on the right-hand side of this door, connected to the redstone circuit inside. Once you've finished placing all of the redstone circuitry inside, cover up your handiwork with plenty of iron blocks.

16

On the left-hand side of the back section you'll need to place a redstone repeater in as part of the of the circuit. Set it to one tick using the small levers. This will change the speed of the doors opening and closing.

17

Now move all around the outside of your build, adding in more iron blocks to cover up the redstone inside and also to give your construct more of an interesting shape. You can always use other blocks, if you like.

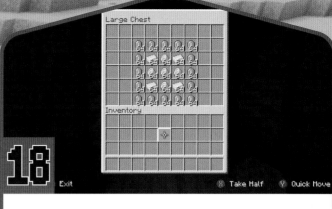

18

With the lever flicked down and the back door open, head inside the build. Open up the chest from the rear and place in any kind of treasure that you like. Make it something that other players will definitely want!

19

Go around to the front of the build again. Now it's time to add a bit more detail. Tempt other players into your trap by placing a sign near the door telling them what sort of loot is inside the treasure chest.

20

Once the sign at the front is done, move to the back of the build and make another one. This will also be placed near the door level, but can always be a bit more mysterious. Will other players choose the right one?

21

To finally complete your build, you can place some decoration on and around the area. We've tried to scare off any potential treasure hunters by adding in skeleton skulls and patches of redstone 'blood'!

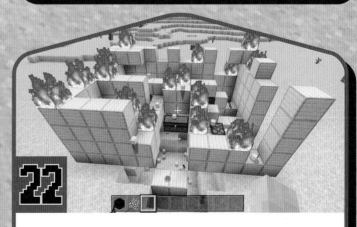

22

Any players that try to walk through the front door to reach the chest will step on the pressure plates and activate the TNT, blowing up the building. Sneaky thieves should definitely try the back door!

TOP 10 MINECRAFT MINI GAMES

While Survival and Creative modes are the main focus of Minecraft, it's also possible to take part in some awesome and fun mini games! These can be played solo or online with friends and there are a bunch of them that are our faves.

1 BATTLE

It's everyone for themselves in this fast-paced mini game! Players compete against each to see who'll be the last one standing. There are over 20 maps to choose from, with weapons, armour, items and loot hidden throughout them.

2 BED WARS

Players start with a single bed and have to build blocks around it as protection from attacking players. Better resources can be purchased from island shops, but going there means leaving your bed unprotected!

3 EGG WARS

Available on the CubeCraft server, this is a fast-paced mini game similar to Bed Wars, but in this mode solo or teams have to defend their egg from enemies. Players also battle over resources such as iron, gold and diamond.

4 BUILD BATTLE

In this mini game, players compete against each other to see who can be the best builder within a set time limit. Players vote on a theme and have to create the best version of that build before showing it off to everyone else.

5 SURVIVAL GAMES

Also known as 'Hunger Games', this is a popular PvP mini game that's also on the CubeCraft server. Similar to Battle, players have to fight against each other to see who'll be the last person left standing.

6 TUMBLE

In this hilarious mini game, players race against the clock to knock each other off a platform into the lava below. This can be done by pushing them off with weapons and items or by removing blocks so they have nothing to stand on.

7 GLIDE

Essentially a flying race, in which players are equipped with elytra wings and have to glide through coloured rings in a variety of levels. There are lots of different maps to race on in Time Attack, Score Attack and Solo modes.

8 ULTRA HARDCORE

This mini game pushes Survival mode to the limit. The aim is to defeat all other players in the level, but your health bar doesn't regenerate naturally. On top of that, you're playing against the clock on a constantly shrinking map.

9 TNT WARS

Another laugh-out-loud mini game, TNT Wars features two teams of players, as they build huge TNT cannons to blow up their opponents. There's nothing more annoying than a massive explosion taking out your build!

10 PARKOUR

This mini game offers players their chance to wall jump their way through a series of challenging maps. The single player mode is tough enough, but multiplayer against the clock is a real test of a gamer's skills!

There's so much to see, do and build in Minecraft, but the game also has a lot of super-secrets to discover that only true fans will know about. Let's take a look at some of these hidden gems, so you can try them out in the game!

MINECRAFT SECRETS

MUSIC DISC GENERATOR

When a skeleton is killed by a creeper with an arrow, the creeper will drop a music disc. Collect the disc and drop it into a jukebox to play some cool tunes! Can you find all of 13 music tracks?

HEROBRINE

A legend amongst Minecraft players, Herobrine is a mythical figure said to be lurking within the game. Whether this elusive character actually exists is up for debate, but some say they have seen him lurking in worlds...

GLIDING ON BLOCKS

Here's a fun trick to try out. Place a slab block on top of any ice blocks and you can then use it to glide on top of the ice. Handy if you've ever wanted to try your hand at skating in Minecraft!

HOLD YOUR BREATH

Did you know there's actually a way to breath underwater? First of all, make sure you have a bucket. Use it underwater and you'll get a 1x1x1 block of air that allows you to breathe forever when submerged.

ROMANTIC VILLAGERS

Under the right circumstances, villagers can fall in love and have little baby villagers. To make that happen, ensure a villager has either 3 x bread, 12 x carrots, 12 x potatoes or 12 x beetroots in one stack of their inventory.

FREE EXTRA WOOL

Paint a sheep a completely different colour before you shear it and it will drop some extra wool. If you're super-lucky, the sheep will drop more than 5 blocks to add to your inventory.

ZAP A PIG

Ever wanted to turn a pig into a zombified piglin? Just make sure a pig is outside during a thunderstorm. If you're lucky it'll get zapped by lightning and transform into a zombified piglin!

HALTING WATER

Water will usually keep flowing unless solid blocks are placed in its path. However, there is another handy way to stop water. Simply place a trapdoor, sign or ladder in front of water and it'll have the same effect.

CURE A ZOMBIE VILLAGER

It is possible to transform a zombified villager back into their regular form if you have the right items. Throw a splash potion of Weakness at the poor villager and then use a golden apple on it and it'll be cured.

BECOME INVISIBLE TO ENDERMEN

When encountering a spooky Enderman, it's best to avoid battling them if possible. To do that, there's a very simple trick to try. Just equip a pumpkin as head armour and you'll be completely invisible to them!

PUZZLES

MINECRAFT WORD SEARCH

Fit all of these Minecraft words into the grid below. You can ignore any spaces in the words – just include the letters. How many can you find?

```
D F A C J P I R Q U H P K S W L
I M O O S H R O O M O R E F R A
E N I R V A E L I G A U L E F P
L T D N U E H N V H J K D R M I
B R Y Z E B R E D V R S E P S S
A A O R G C T W U E T O R H O L
T W D J O N R K O O R O G M U A
G R F Y L P Q A N R T M U T L Z
N E D H D R B E F S L P A J S U
I H G U E Z F A E T Y D R N A L
T T H E N E T H E R R R T D F N I
F E K R A M H W Q B O E I R D Y
A N V U P D A T E A Q U A T I C
R Q O C P E U F G I L O N L S D
C S I B L T A M E D W O L F M P
N E N D E R D R A G O N G A R S
```

THE NETHER	MOOSHROOM	NETHER WART
OVERWORLD	ENDER DRAGON	CRAFTING TABLE
MINECRAFT REALMS	ELDER GUARDIAN	TAMED WOLF
GOLDEN APPLE	REDSTONE	SOUL SAND
LAPIS LAZULI	ENDERMAN	UPDATE AQUATIC

FIND THE DIAMONDS

Use the coordinates at the top and side of the grid to work out the correct square that the diamond is in. Write your answer in the space below.

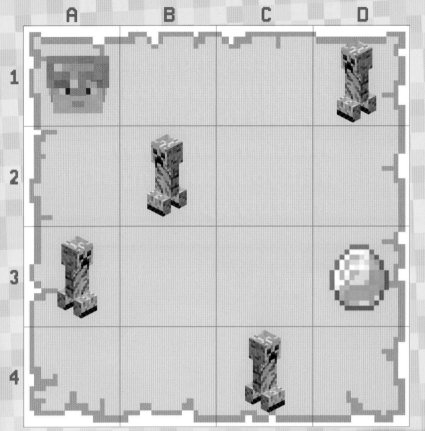

GUESS THE SKINS

These two images of Minecraft skins have been mixed up and combined into one. Look closely and see if you can work out which two skins they are.

NAME THE MOB

Can you name each of the mobs above, just from their heads? Take a close look and write the answers below each image.

Answers on p76

BUILD #5

TOTAL TOWER DEFENCE

For the final build, we're going to construct a classic Minecraft tower, complete with hidden defences and features. Once finished you'll be able to take on all attackers and prove that your building skills are truly epic!

1

Create a new world to begin making your tower. We've decided to place ours in an extreme hills biome. This not only makes it look really cool, but it also helps to blend the tower into the landscape.

2

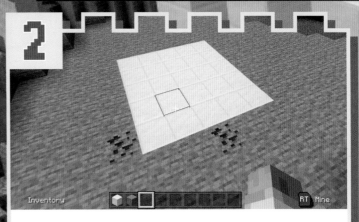

Find or clear a flat area to start construction. For this build we're going to mark out the area with a square of 5x5 quartz blocks. You can always make your tower much bigger though, but it will take longer.

3

Next, move on to the tower's walls. Keep adding quartz blocks all around each side to make them higher. It's also a good idea at this stage to leave a space for a main entrance and any windows you might want.

4

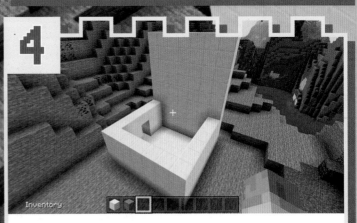

Finish adding blocks until the first floor walls are three blocks high. Once that's done, add more blocks to each wall to increase the overall height of the tower. We're going to make the full height 12 blocks.

5

Head to the roof and add a smooth stone floor and battlements. These should be 2 blocks high and go all around the top of the tower. These battlements will be a great place to shoot arrows from too!

6

What would a tower be without a defensive moat? This build has that, but we've added in lava instead of water! The moat is two blocks wide so that attackers will meet a fiery end if they try to jump over it.

7

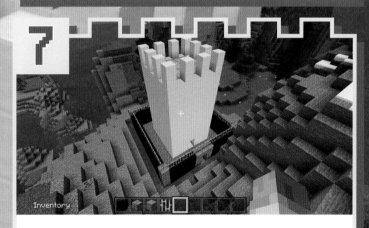

Around the lava moat, make a solid wall from obsidian blocks and stone blocks. This will be very tough for players to break through and can be topped off with iron bars for a truly medieval look!

8

For your tower's first hidden defence, we're going to try something that might seem a little bit unusual. To start, remove a block on either side of the main entrance and pour in a bucket of pufferfish.

9

On the wall above the pufferfish, place a sticky piston with a lever on it. Repeat the same setup on the wall on the other side of the entrance. Flick the levers down, then break both sticky piston blocks.

10

Finally, place a single stone block on top of where each pufferfish is in the ground. It may now look like there isn't anything there, but if players walk between the blocks they'll be poisoned and die!

11 For the next defence, head inside the tower entrance and look back where you came from. You'll want to dig down under the stone path into your build and place a single sticky piston below the blocks.

12 Cover the first piston up with a stone block to hide it. Now add another sticky piston and hide that one with a stone block too. From the outside, no one should be able to tell there's anything hidden there.

13 From inside your tower, tunnel down and carve out a space near the hidden sticky pistons. Then you'll need to add blocks, redstone torches, redstone repeaters and redstone dust on top of blocks as shown.

14 Add more stone blocks across from your redstone circuit to the ground level above. These should also have redstone dust on top of them. Make sure you don't miss any out, or the circuit won't work.

15 Come out of the hole you've made and add a lever on the right-hand side of the entrance in your tower. Make sure you place it in the correct spot so that it links up to the hidden redstone circuit below.

16 Cover up any holes left in the floor with quartz blocks to hide the mechanism. Test out your build by flicking the lever to raise a secret drawbridge! This is another great way of stopping players getting inside.

17

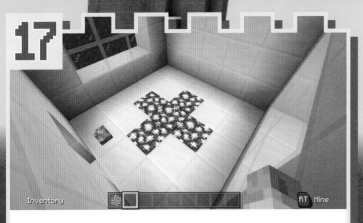

Now it's time to do more work to the tower's interior. Place glowstone blocks in the floor to light the place up. You can also take out quartz blocks from the wall to make windows and add in glass panes.

18

To reach the upper levels of the tower, try adding in an impressive spiral staircase. This can be made from smooth stone blocks and slabs placed one next to the other, twisting all the way up to the roof.

19

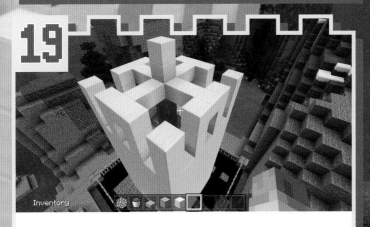

Complete the top of the tower with more quartz blocks as shown. If you add water inside the very centre block and then cover it up, you'll have a very cool waterfall feature running down the spiral staircase!

20

To protect the top of the tower from sneaky flying attackers, add a simple dispenser with a lever on it. Inside place coloured fireworks and flick the lever down. Anyone trying to land will be blown up!

21

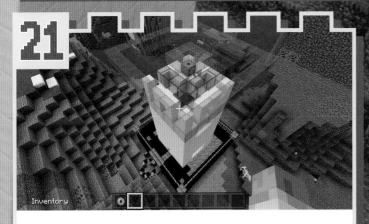

For a final decorative effect, use light blue, dark blue and cyan glass blocks around the top of the tower. This adds a great finishing touch and makes it look like blue energy is radiating out from the roof.

22

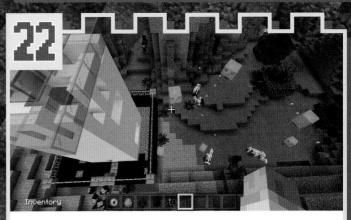

Now test out your tower's awesome defensive capabilities by spawning all sorts of hostile mobs around the base. Even if they don't manage to make it inside, they might also scare off any attacking players!

THE ULTIMATE MINECRAFT QUIZ

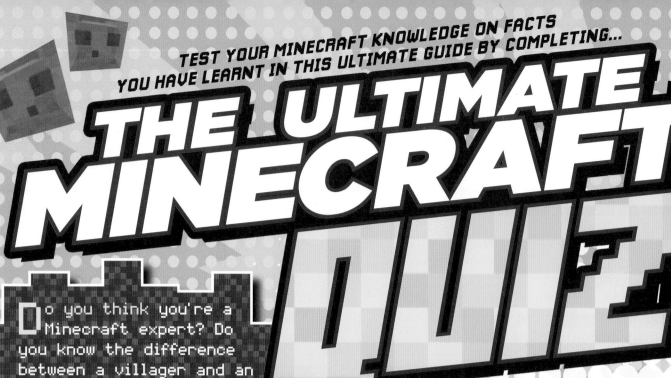

Do you think you're a Minecraft expert? Do you know the difference between a villager and an illager or how many iron blocks you need to make a golem? Then challenge yourself and see how many of these tricky questions you can answer correctly!

1 Which biome is made of hardened clay, red sand and trees?

2 Where can Netherrack, glowstone and soul sand blocks be found?

3 What is the name of the service that allows players to create servers?

4 Which blocks are impossible to destroy in Survival?

5 What substance is used to create circuits in Minecraft?

6 Where are sponge blocks to be found?

7 What's the name of the mythical character said to be hiding in the game?

8 Which block should you wear on your head to hide from an Enderman?

9

What's the name of the currency used in the Minecraft Marketplace?

10

What prize do you get for completing the End?

11

Which items does the Wither drop?

12

Which famous Minecraft YouTuber's real name is Joseph Garrett?

13

On which server would you play Egg Wars?

14

What rare mob might appear when you throw an Ender pearl?

15

What is the name of the company that created Minecraft?

16

What does the light level need to be less than for growing mushrooms?

17

What will a pig turn into if it's struck by lightning?

18

How many obsidian blocks do you need to build a Nether portal?

19

What's the rarest colour of sheep?

20

What are the game's two basic starter skins?

YOUR QUIZ RATING

0-5
You're probably safer staying in the Overworld and brushing up on your mining skills.

5-10
With a few good builds under belt, you're ready to take on tough mobs below ground.

10-15
Your survival and creative abilities are growing and your inventory is full of cool items.

15-20
Congratulations! You've beaten every Minecraft challenge and become an expert builder.

Answers on p76

TOP 10
MINECRAFT
YOUTUBERS

There are all sorts of amazing Minecraft YouTube videos that are worth checking out if you need any hints, tips or inspiration for your own epic builds. These YouTubers are some of the biggest Minecraft fans in the world and their channels have millions of dedicated subscribers!

1 PAUL SOARES JR.

YouTube Profile: poulsooresjr

Gamer, husband and dad, this YouTuber has plenty of family-friendly videos on his channel that are well-worth watching. He specialises in content for newcomers to Minecraft, offering straightforward Let's Plays, tutorials and how to information.

Best videos:
Newbies should definitely watch Paul's essential *How to Survive* and *Thrive* tutorials for simple step-by-step builds.

2 STAMPY

YouTube Profile: stampylonghead

Also known as Mr. Stampy Cat (aka Joseph Garrett), this long-time Minecraft gamer posts fun Let's Plays and handy tutorial videos on his channel. He currently has over 9 million subscribers who regularly tune in for his live streams and game challenges.

Best videos:
Noobs and younger gamers should check out Stampy's *How To Minecraft* series to get started.

3 IBALLISTICSQUID

YouTube Profile: iBallisticSquid

As a cartoon cat, Stampy's best friend is obviously a squid! Popping up in Stampy's videos from time to time, Squiddy (or Squid Nugget aka David Spencer) uploads his own Let's Plays, mods and video challenges, often set for him by Stampy.

Best videos:

If you're looking for mods to try, take a look at Squiddy's excellent *Pixelmon Learning the Basics* videos.

4 THEATLANTICCRAFT

YouTube Profile: TheAtlanticCraft

Hardcore Minecraft gamers should go watch the YouTube channel created by Cody (theCodyMaverick) and Joe (JoeBuzz). Their Let's Plays, mods and mini-games are more advanced and tons of fun.

Best videos:

For top laughs, you have to see the 'Let It Glow' video, a hilarious parody of the song 'Let It Go', from Disney's *Frozen*!

5 CAPTAINSPARKLEZ

YouTube Profile: CaptainSparklez

With over 10 million subscribers, CaptainSparklez offers his fans technically-advanced worlds and even parody videos. Definitely one for more experienced Minecraft players to watch, as jargon can get a little complicated.

Best videos:

For an epic adventure packed with dungeons, dimensions and tough-as-nails enemies, take a look at his *Super Modded Survival Series*.

6 LITTLE LIZARD GAMING
YouTube Profile: Little Lizard Adventures

This popular YouTube channel is run by Irish brothers, Ryan and Scott Fitzimons. Here you'll find Minecraft game play-throughs, how-tos and mods videos, that are very funny. This channel is also 100% kid-friendly, so perfect for families.

Best videos:

Check out Little Lizard Gaming's *Minecraft Pixelmon Mod*, a hilarious mix of Pokémon and Minecraft!

7 PRESTONPLAYZ
YouTube Profile: Preston

This gamer and vlogger has over 13 million subscribers worldwide! His awesome Minecraft videos are aimed more at players that are familiar with the basics, but want to start to expand their building skills.

Best videos:

Preston's parkour maps are the stuff of legend and his secrets of Minecraft videos are a must-watch too.

8 MINECRAFT UNIVERSE
YouTube Profile: Minecraft Universe

There is loads of great content on this channel, which is hosted by TrueMU (aka Jason Probst), who's also in a Minecraft gaming group called Team Crafted. His channel is packed with awesome adventure maps, parkour maps, mini-games and more.

Best videos:

The mods, Top 10s, secrets, facts and glitches videos are cool and TrueMU even makes his own Minecraft music videos!

9 THE BAJAN CANADIAN

YouTube Profile: Bajan Canadian

For older fans of Minecraft, The Bajan Canadian (aka Mitchell Hughes) has a wide range of videos on his channel. Although more on the technical side, they're still fun to watch as he delivers them with gentle nerdy humour.

Best videos:

Check out The Bajan Canadian's crazy parkour maps and lightning-fast speedruns through levels. This guy can really move!

10 THEDIAMONDMINECRAFT

YouTube Profile: DanTDM

The king of YouTube gaming, Dan's channel has over a whopping 22 million subscribers worldwide! Aimed mostly at more experienced gamers, there are videos on everything from Let's Plays and mod reviews to challenges and secret worlds.

Best videos:

Watch TheDiamondMinecraft take on fellow YouTuber Stampy and friends in the epic Hunger Games-style Egypt map!

Also check out:

ETHOSLAB

YouTube Profile: EthosLab

Take a look at his popular series, *Etho Plays Minecraft*, where he makes incredible Redstone constructs.

MARICRAFT

YouTube Profile: Maricraft

You have to watch the *Splegg in Your Face!* videos, in which Mari and friends throw spleggs (Minecraft eggs) at each other!

POPULAR MMOS

YouTube Profile: Popular MMOs

In honour of their cat passing away, Pat and Jen battle it out against each other in the epic *Minecraft Kitty Cat Challenge*.

THINKNOODLES

YouTube Profile: Thinknoodles

There are all kinds of great Minecraft videos on here, but they all share one thing in common: his golden retriever, Kopi!

SETH BLING

YouTube Profile: SethBling

A Redstone expert, Sethbling makes great Minecraft tutorials on things like how to fry an egg and build a Minecraft washing machine!

PUZZLE ANSWERS

Page 24
MOB SHADOWS

1	2	3	4	5
Creeper	Witch	Zombie	Shulker	Ghast

SLIME SPOT THE DIFFERENCE

Page 25
MIXED-UP MOBS

HROOMMOOS = MOOSHROOM
GAVLRLEI = VILLAGER
KLRESUH = SHULKER
NROI LGMOE = IRON GOLEM
RAPLO AREB = POLAR BEAR
NNADREEM = ENDERMAN
YBBA BZEMIO = BABY ZOMBIE
RELDE NGRAUIDA = ELDER GUARDIAN
THE RWTHEI = THE WITHER
RENED RANDGO = ENDER DRAGON

MISSING BLOCKS

MINECRAFT MAZE

Page 37
HIDDEN HEROBRINE

BLOCK SEQUENCE

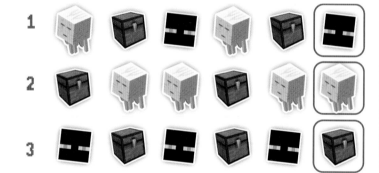

TOO MANY CHICKENS!

There are 32 chickens in the picture

Page 46
DISTORTED BIOMES

(A) ICE PLAINS
(B) MUSHROOM ISLAND
(C) MESA
(D) DESERT

CRAFTING RECIPES

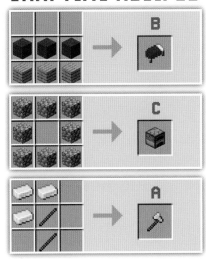

Page 47

WHICH WITCH?

Witch 3 is the odd one out.

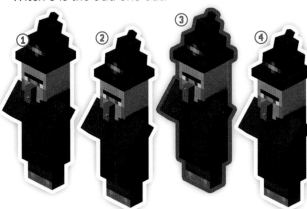

MOB MEMORY GAME

1. There are five torches

2. The brown dirt blocks are on the left of the picture

3. There are only one of the spider and Enderman mobs

4. Two zombie faces can be seen

Page 64

MINECRAFT WORD SEARCH

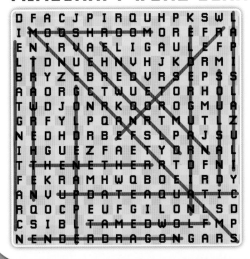

Page 65

FIND THE DIAMONDS

The diamond is in square D3

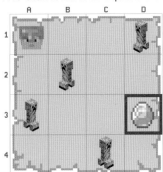

GUESS THE SKINS

The skins are Bob The Builder and Batman

NAME THE MOB

Zombie Villager   Wandering Trader

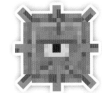

Enderman   Mooshroom   Guardian

Page 70 - 71

THE ULTIMATE MINECRAFT QUIZ

1. Mesa
2. The Nether
3. Minecraft Realms Plus
4. Bedrock
5. Redstone
6. Underwater
7. Herobrine
8. Pumpkin
9. Minecoins
10. 12,000 XP and Dragon egg
11. Ghast tear and gunpowder
12. Mr. Stampy Cat
13. CubeCraft
14. Endermite
15. Mojang
16. Less than 12
17. Zombified piglin
18. 10
19. Pink
20. Steve and Alex

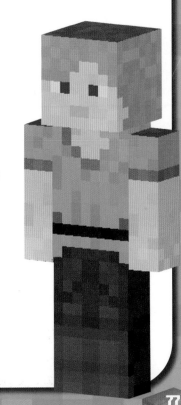